THE IRISH LITERARY MOVEMENT

A. Norman Jeffares

NPG

Published in Great Britain by National Portrait Gallery Publications,
National Portrait Gallery, St Martin's Place, London WC2H 0HE

ISBN 1 85514 233 3

A catalogue record for this book is available from the British Library

Series Project Editors: Celia Jones and Lucy Clark
Series Picture Researcher: Susie Foster
Series Designer: Karen Osborne
Printed by PJ Reproductions, London

Front cover
James Joyce, 1882–1941
Jacques-Emile Blanche, 1935 (detail)
Oil on canvas, 125.1 x 87.6 cm
© National Portrait Gallery (3883)

For a complete catalogue of current publications,
please write to the address above.

CONTENTS

JAMES JOYCE, Jacques-Emile Blanche, 1935

INTRODUCTION

❧

This book represents some of the many writers whose work makes up the Irish literary movement and its development into contemporary Irish writing. They were part of a remarkable outburst of creative energy, literary and linguistic, artistic and political, which occurred towards the end of the nineteenth century, when a rapidly increasing number of Irish people wanted to explore and affirm their Irish identity. The roots of the movement went back to late-eighteenth century antiquarianism with its studies of Irish history, antiquities, music and poetry.

Standish O'Grady (1846–1928), regarded as the father of the literary movement, became a populariser of the old Gaelic romances, producing 'the splendour' of his own *History of Ireland: The Heroic Period* in 1878. Delighted by this and O'Grady's other writings, especially *Cuchulain: An Epic* (1882), W. B. Yeats (1865–1939), who gave the literary movement its impetus and initial direction, realised that Gaelic legends and mythology, combined with the fairy and folk tales he encountered in Co. Sligo, provided exciting new Irish subject-matter.

Yeats's aim, to blend this Gaelic material with the best of English literary tradition and techniques, was paralleled by that of Douglas Hyde (1860–1949), who, unlike Yeats, had learned Irish and passionately wished to keep the language alive, publishing his own poems in it as well as excellent translations of Irish tales and poems put into effective Hiberno-English, the English spoken in former Irish-speaking areas. The two men aided each other, Hyde becoming President of the National Literary Society founded by Yeats in 1892.

In the latter part of the nineteenth century the political temperature rose in Ireland. The Irish Republican Brotherhood (IRB), a clandestine nationalist organisation, was founded in 1858. The Fenian disturbances of 1867 were followed by the movement for Home Rule, which began in 1870 and had sixty Irish Home Rule MPs in Westminster by 1874. From 1880 the Irish Parliamentary Party led by Charles Stewart Parnell (1846–91) held the balance of power at Westminster. The Land Wars, which involved tenants withholding rents, led to the Land Acts (which, in effect, ultimately changed Ireland into a country of small farmers), the Ashbourne Act of 1885 and the Wyndham Act of 1903, which gave Treasury loans to tenants to buy out their landlords. Gladstone took up Home

Rule, but both his bills were defeated. Parnell died in 1891 and the ensuing vacuum in Irish politics seemed to Yeats the time to launch a literary revival.

This literary revival had many of its roots in Dublin, a suitable vat for the intellectual ferment the revival engendered, for it was a city not unlike classical Athens in the cross currents and intimacy of its cultural life. It was indeed a closely knit society with personal links between the worlds of music, art and literature, something well suggested by the Irish artist Sir William Orpen (1878–1931) in a sketch of 1907. This portrays Sir Hugh Lane (1875–1915), Lady Gregory's nephew, who founded the Municipal Gallery of Modern Art in Dublin, and three directors of the Abbey Theatre from 1905, John Millington Synge (1871–1909), W. B. Yeats and Lady Gregory (1852–1932). Several Irish writers began with the aim of becoming artists: George Moore (1852–1933), Yeats, George Russell (1867–1935) and Edith Somerville (1858–1949). Lady Gregory painted and drew well, while the artist Sarah Purser (1849–1953) and the caricaturist Isa MacNie (?1869/70–1958) were friends of many of the writers. Dublin was a musical city, with its concerts, music halls and musical evenings, something that was well brought out in his fiction by James Joyce (1882–1941).

Some Irish men and women, then, well aware of foreign and avant-garde movements, wanted to share their consciousness of them and of past Gaelic culture with their contemporaries, although in doing so they had to struggle with fiercely opposing views. Not for nothing did George Moore quote George Russell as saying that a literary movement consisted of five or six people who live in one town and hate each other cordially.

Something of the intense literary activity occurring at varying levels in Ireland is conveyed in Moore's *Hail and Farewell* (1911–14), Joyce's *Dubliners* (1914) and Oliver St John Gogarty's (1878–1957) *As I was going down Sackville Street* (1937). There were arguments in plenty – between establishment Unionists and Nationalists, though both could dislike (for different reasons) the dedication and persistence of the new writers, critics and patrons who were departing from stereotyped views of Irish life, whether Unionist or Nationalist.

It was not without occasional acrimony also that the Irish theatre came into being. The Irish Literary Theatre was the name Yeats gave it in 1899;

LADY ISABELLA AUGUSTA GREGORY, SIR HUGH LANE, JOHN MILLINGTON SYNGE AND WILLIAM BUTLER YEATS, Sir William Orpen, 1907

its first plays were produced in Dublin and it lasted until 1901, when it was succeeded by the National Theatre Society, incorporating the Irish National Dramatic Company run by the amateur actor W. G. Fay (1871–1931). Yeats's English friend Miss Annie Horniman (1860–1937) bought the Mechanics Institute Theatre in Abbey Street, Dublin, which became the Abbey Theatre. It opened in 1904 with Fay as manager, and from 1905 the theatre was run by three directors, Yeats, Lady Gregory and Synge.

A nationalist backlash against the new literary movement developed, exemplified in rioting against Synge's *The Playboy of the Western World* in 1907, something which recurred at the production of Sean O'Casey's (1880–1964) *The Plough and the Stars* in 1927. This arose out of the attitudes of the 'Irish-Irelanders' led by D. P. Moran (1869–1936), a polemical author, proprietor and editor of *The Leader* newspaper from 1900, who thought true Irishness could only be Gaelic and Catholic. The Irish-Irelanders were suspicious of the many, mainly Protestant, Anglo-Irish writers, such as Yeats, Lady Gregory and Synge. Despite his commitment to the Irish language, Douglas Hyde had to tread carefully to avoid antagonising extreme nationalist feelings. Of course, the Anglo-Irish writers were themselves rebelling against their own heritage with their vision of a regenerated and unified Ireland proud of its past.

GEORGE MOORE, Sir William Orpen

Paradoxically, it was Catholic writers of fiction – for example, George Moore and James Joyce – who showed Ireland a realistic picture of itself. Much Irish drama, initially heroic and poetic, rapidly became realistic as the Abbey Theatre got into its stride; the realists, who included Padraic Colum (1881–1972) and William Boyle (1853–1922), had followed the lead given earlier by Edward Martyn (1859–1923), a Catholic landlord and co-founder of the Irish Literary Theatre, in his Ibsen-like plays on contemporary life.

W. B. YEATS, Howard Coster, 1935

The course of the revival was not smoothly progressive. Writers developed, changed their views. Yeats, once in the revolutionary IRB (which was revived in the early twentieth century), became a conservative admirer of aristocracy. Standish O'Grady, a Unionist, had, however, foretold that the cultural revolution would be followed by a military one. He was right. A Home Rule Bill was finally passed by the Commons in 1914, but by then opposition in Ulster to Home Rule had led to the creation of the armed force of Ulster Volunteers in 1913, countered by the National Volunteers in the south. The Lords amended the Bill to exclude Ulster, then the Bill was suspended because of the outbreak of the First World War. Large numbers of Irishmen joined the British forces, although a minority remained strongly opposed to British rule in Ireland and became associated with the nationalist Sinn Fein movement (*Sinn Fein* means Ourselves, or Ourselves Alone) led by Arthur Griffith (1871–1922). A decision to embark upon the 1916 Easter Rising was taken, but the rebellion was put down, and its fifteen leaders executed, becoming political martyrs. This swung support behind Sinn Fein, which triumphed in the 1918 General Election. There followed the so-called Anglo-Irish War between British forces and the Irish Republican Army, from 1919 to 1921 when a truce was called and the Treaty of 1922 created the twenty-six county

S<small>EAN</small> O'C<small>ASEY</small>
Elliott & Fry, 17 January 1934

Irish Free State (the six northern counties had been given a Parliament in 1920). The new Free State Government had to face a civil war – Eamon de Valera (1882–1972) leading the anti-Treaty forces in a violent campaign for a thirty-two county independent Ireland – until peace was restored in 1923.

To return to literary matters is to realise how George Moore, an enthusiast for the revival, became disillusioned and left Dublin in 1911 for London. His house in Co. Mayo was later burnt down in the Civil War. O'Casey too settled in England, in 1929, as did George Russell in 1933, who said he disliked living in an Ireland 'run by louts'.

They were to be followed, in disillusion, by some of the new generation of fiction writers, themselves formerly involved in revolutionary guerrilla activities: Eimar O'Duffy (1893–1935), Sean O'Faolain (1900–91), Frank O'Connor (1903–66) and Liam O'Flaherty (1896–1984). The new Irish Free State was not what they hoped for, and their tough, even brutally realistic views of the nature of Irish life were unwelcome in a highly conservative, largely Catholic-controlled southern Ireland, with its puritan Censorship of Publications Act of 1929, the effects of which were not undone until the virtual abolition of the original Act in 1967. Criticism of de Valera's concept of Ireland as a family-centred rural community of small farmers, based on a Gaelic Catholic nation, came from many, and included the anti-pastoral writings of Patrick Kavanagh (1904–1967), notably his poem *The Great Hunger* (1942). Patrick Kavanagh is not represented here, nor is Austin Clarke (1896–1974), yet they were the main Irish poets who succeeded Yeats. The reason is that, as its name suggests, the National Portrait Gallery does not imply a collection of non-British portraits. It is not surprising then that it does not include Kavanagh and

Clarke as sitters, nor, say, Oliver St John Gogarty, Frank O'Connor or Mary Lavin (1912–96). There is, however, an impressive holding of portraits of authors born and bred in an Ireland all of which was part of the United Kingdom, images both of those who shaped the literary movement, such as Yeats, Russell and Moore, and of those who were either not directly or closely associated with it, such as George Bernard Shaw or, later, Joyce Cary (1888–1957).

The Gallery's philosophy, however, is not narrowly restrictive, for we find in it writers up to our own time, from James Joyce, through Sean O'Faolain and Kate O'Brien (1897–1974) to Seamus Heaney (b. 1939), whose roots lie outside Britain. In acquiring portraits the Trustees have taken a broader approach; considering the significance of a sitter's contribution, they have provided the Collection with many portraits of men and women who have played an influential role in the literary, cultural or historical life of the nation within as well as beyond the United Kingdom's boundaries.

The strength of the literary movement's achievement can be measured today by its capacity to contain various kinds of mockery and self-mockery. Thus, Samuel Beckett (1906–89), while being an early admirer and explicator of Joyce's elaboration, reacted strongly against twilight, heroic Celticism. Beckett was himself to bring minimalism to the Irish repertoire, while Joyce's successor, Flann O'Brien (1911–66), another sharp parodist, could mock at both Gaelic and Anglo-Irish traditions while establishing his own darkly satiric comedy.

By the 1950s the complexities, the opposites even, of the literary movement had reached a resolution: Irish writers could, simply, be themselves; so now there is an infinite variety of writing from authors well aware of their complex inheritance but contributing their own subject-matter, attitudes and styles.

Some of the long-established themes, however, live on. That of the Big House was begun by Maria Edgeworth (1767–1849) in *Castle Rackrent* (1800), the first regional novel in English. The Big Houses provided topics of extravagance, arrogance, improvidence and anxiety in the decline of the landowning largely Protestant Ascendancy; these could also provide dramatic contrasts with the poverty of the peasantry. The theme was developed by Somerville (1858–1949) and Ross (1862–1915), and con-

11

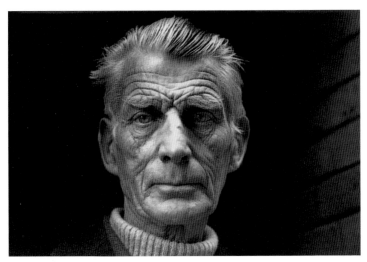

S<small>AMUEL</small> B<small>ECKETT</small>, Jane Bown, 1976

tinued in some of the writings of Elizabeth Bowen (1899–1973) and Joyce Cary, and has inspired some of the arrestingly brilliant fiction of William Trevor (b. 1928), and the evocative novels of Jennifer Johnston (b. 1930) or John Banville (b. 1945). Northern clarity, first emergent in St John Ervine's (1883–1971) plays about Belfast or in the prose of Forrest Reid (1875–1947), also drives the wide-ranging novels of Brian Moore (b. 1921) or the impressive, searching drama of Brian Friel (b. 1929), while the poetry of Brendan Kennelly (b. 1936) and Seamus Heaney, country-men both, reflects their unique approaches to contemporary Irish life.

Traditions founded upon early Gaelic literature or the literature in English that began with Jonathan Swift are there for Irish writers to con-tinue or to depart from at their will. One thing, however, remains certain: the literary skills continue. Not for nothing have the Nobel Prizes awarded to Yeats and Shaw in the twenties been followed by those awarded to Beckett and Heaney in our time. Contemporary Irish writers are the grown-up children of the literary movement.

SELECT BIBLIOGRAPHY

B. Arnold, *A Concise History of Irish Art*, Thames & Hudson, London (2nd rev. ed.), 1977.

E. Boyd, *Ireland's Literary Renaissance*, Figgis, Dublin (rev. ed.), 1965.

P. Boylan, *All Cultivated People: A History of the United Arts Club, Dublin*, Colin Smythe, Gerrards Cross, 1988.

N. Corcoran, *After Yeats and Joyce. Reading Modern Irish Literature*, Oxford University Press, 1997.

P. Costello, *The Heart Grown Brutal: The Irish Revolution in Literature, from Parnell to the Death of Yeats, 1891–1939*, Gill & MacMillan, Dublin, 1978.

A. Crookshank and the Knight of Glin, *The Painters of Ireland, c.1600–1920*, Barrie & Jenkins, London, 1978.

M. and C. Cruise O'Brien, *Ireland: A Concise History*, Thames & Hudson, London (3rd ed. rev.), 1985.

J. W. Foster, *Fictions of the Irish Literary Revival: A Changeling Act*, Gill & MacMillan, Dublin, 1987.

R. F. Foster, *Modern Ireland, 1600–1972*, Allen Lane, The Penguin Press, London, 1988.

E. Healy, *Literary Tour of Ireland*, Wolfhound Press, Dublin, 1995.

H. Howarth, *The Irish Writers, 1880–1940*, Hill & Wang, New York, 1959.

B. Inglis, *The Story of Ireland*, Faber & Faber, London (2nd ed. rev.), 1965.

A. N. Jeffares, *A History of Anglo-Irish Literature*, Macmillan, London, 1982.

A. N. Jeffares, *A Pocket History of Irish Literature*, O'Brien Press, Dublin, 1997.

F. S. L. Lyons, *Ireland Since the Famine*, Fontana, London (2nd rev. ed.), 1973.

G. Moore, *Hail and Farewell* [*Ave*, *Salve* and *Vale* in one volume], (ed. Richard Cave) Colin Smythe, Gerrards Cross, 1976.

F. O'Connor, *A Backward Look: A Survey of Irish Literature*, Macmillan, London, 1967.

W. R. Rodgers, *Irish Literary Portraits*, BBC, London, 1972.

W. Trevor, *A Writer's Ireland*, Thames & Hudson, London, 1984.

N. Vance, *Irish Literature: A Social History*, Basil Blackwell, Oxford, 1990.

R. Welch (ed.), *Oxford Companion to Irish Literature*, Oxford University Press, 1996.

W. B. Yeats, *Autobiographies*, Macmillan, London, 1955.

W. B. Yeats, *Essays and Introductions*, Macmillan, London, 1961.

STANDISH JAMES O'GRADY (1846–1928)

The son of a rector in Co. Cork, O'Grady, a barrister and leader-writer on the conservative *Dublin Daily Express*, came across Sylvester O'Halloran's *Introduction to the Study of the History and Antiquities of Ireland* (1778) on a wet afternoon in a country house. It inflamed his interest in Irish literature, developed further by reading Eugene O'Curry's *Customs and Manners of the Ancient Irish* (1873). O'Grady's own first book, a two volume *History of Ireland: The Heroic Period* (1878), was the text that sparked off the literary revival.

O'Grady knew no Irish but skilfully arranged and condensed his sources. He gave heroic status to the men and women in his Irish tales, seeking to convey the grandeur of Irish myth and legend and make the Irish past an inspiration for the present. His style, a blend of Walter Scott, Thomas Carlyle and the King James Bible, conveyed 'all events in blazing torchlight'. Two other histories were followed by *Cuchulain: An Epic* (1882).

O'Grady came to think that the landlord class was finished unless it saved Ireland from materialism by providing leadership for its Gaelic people and inspiring them with a sense of the continuity of Irish history – a vain hope for an escape from its apparent paralysis. He put forward these views in the *Dublin Daily Express*, then in the *Kilkenny Moderator*, which he bought and edited, and later in the *All Ireland Review*, which he founded and ran from 1900 to 1905.

John Butler Yeats conveys O'Grady's straightforward manner, but he only hints at his capacity for passionate quarrelling. Frustrated and disillusioned, O'Grady left Ireland in 1918, dying in the Isle of Wight in 1928. His vigorous, romantic writing appealed to his readers, and his linking of the mythological hero Cuchulain's leadership with Ireland's destiny had a profound effect on the intellectual and emotional climate of the revival.

Standish O'Grady

STANDISH JAMES O'GRADY, John Butler Yeats, 1907

SIR SAMUEL FERGUSON (1810–86)

❧

Unlike O'Grady, Ferguson had a good knowledge of Irish and, wanting to make past culture more readily available, proved himself an excellent translator of short Irish poems, conveying the energy and power of the originals.

The shorter poems of his *Lays of the Western Gael and Other Poems* (1865) were followed by longer poems that gave accurate treatment of heroic legends: the epic *Congal* (1872), and *Deirdre's Lament for the Sons of Usnach* (1864) are the best, although 'The Welshmen of Tirawley' (1845) shows Ferguson's capacity to re-create the toughness of his originals. His work lacked a sensuous quality, perhaps the reason why he was less effective than O'Grady.

Born in Belfast, educated there, at Lincoln's Inn and at Trinity College, Dublin, Ferguson became Deputy Keeper of the Records and President of the Royal Irish Academy. A good scholar, a fluent speaker of Latin and a careful archaeologist, his own poetry, notably his 'Lament for Thomas Davis', proved effective in its Keatsian use of compound words.

As well as being a poet and a critic with a capacity for comic writing Ferguson was by nature a political conciliator who wanted to bridge gaps between the Protestant Ascendancy and the rest of the country, while realising the difficulties. He put them very clearly early in his life, in 1833, in 'A Dialogue between the Head and the Heart of an Irish Protestant', published in the *Dublin University Magazine*. His own ambition was to do what he could in 'the formation of a characteristic school of letters for my own country'.

The Dublin painter Sarah Purser's vigorous posthumous portrait, taken from a photograph, conveys Samuel Ferguson's innate sense of humour, while suggesting the strains imposed by his incessant hard work.

SIR SAMUEL FERGUSON, Sarah Purser, 1888

WILLIAM BUTLER YEATS (1865–1939)

O'Grady and Ferguson showed Yeats the way to Gaelic legend and mythology, which he combined with his interest in the scenery and fairy and folk tales of Co. Sligo, where he had spent much of his childhood. His father, always short of money, moved his family between Dublin and London, where Willie Yeats did not enjoy his English school, feeling that English attitudes were not for him. In Dublin again, he went to the High School, then to the School of Art where he and George Russell became friends, sharing an interest in mysticism and the supernatural. Yeats decided to become a writer and his early verse reflects English romantic poetry, but *The Wanderings of Oisin* (1889) established the tone of what became known as the 'Celtic Twilight'. His love poetry was idealistic, beautiful, adjectival, shadowy, melancholic and defeatist.

Yeats emerged from his Protestant background into knowledge of an Irish Catholic world in 1885, when he became friendly with Katharine Tynan, through whom he met editors of Irish periodicals. In 1889 he met and fell in love with Maud Gonne (1866–1953), remaining obsessed by this spectacularly beautiful woman for much of his life. A strong supporter of Irish nationalism in speeches, journalism and political campaigns, she consistently refused his proposals of marriage and in 1903 married John MacBride (1868–1916). Yeats remained on friendly terms with Maud, and continued to write love poems to and about her.

Yeats grew up in a milieu where art, discussion and criticism were natural, necessary activities. (Not only was his father an artist, but his brother Jack B. Yeats (1871–1957) was to become Ireland's foremost painter.) As a result there are many paintings, drawings and photographs of William. They reveal not only something of his dreamy nature (as in his father's portrait of him), but his determination to develop a distinctive, distinguished Irish literature that drove him into much activity: journalism propagandising the new Irish writing, the foundation of two literary societies, compilations of Irish fairy tales, selections from Irish novelists, and books of Irish verse.

In 1897 Yeats spent the first of his summer stays at Coole Park, Lady Gregory's house in Co. Galway. She joined him in the intense work that resulted in the creation of the Abbey Theatre in 1904, which involved him in battles against hostility not only to his plays but those of Synge too.

WILLIAM BUTLER YEATS, John Butler Yeats, 1907

By the end of the century Yeats had changed his elaborate prose and decorative symbolist poetry, and began to write in a more direct, powerful, even bitter style. The years 1916–17 were crucial for him. John MacBride was one of the leaders shot after the Easter Rising (about which Yeats wrote so tellingly in 'Easter 1916', realising the leaders had become martyrs) and Yeats proposed yet again to Maud. As usual she refused him.

WILLIAM BUTLER YEATS
Kathleen Scott, 1907

He then proposed to her daughter Iseult by Lucien Millevoye, but, on her also refusing him, in 1917 he married a young Englishwoman, Georgie Hyde Lees, whom he had known since 1911. Marriage gave Yeats a self-confidence which surged through the poems he now wrote about historical change and the decay and possible destruction of western civilisation (in such hauntingly disturbing poems as 'The Second Coming', written in 1919).

Yeats's dreams now eventuated in reality: marriage, children and a possible base in Ireland (a medieval castle in Co. Galway, the tower bought for £35 in 1917). To the castle was added a fine town house in Dublin, suitable residence for the Senator of the Irish Free State that Yeats, the erstwhile revolutionary nationalist, had now become. Then followed the award of the Nobel Prize for Literature in 1923. The poems of *The Tower* (1928) and *The Winding Stair* (1933) showed a blend of beauty and harshness, allusive, outspoken and emotive in their romantic rhetoric, magisterial in their questioning, even into his old age. His *Last Poems and Two Plays* (1939) testify to his continuing poetic passions, an old man's frenzy to arrange everything in one clear view.

Yeats was often drawn, painted and photographed. Augustus John portrayed him as a bohemian (which he was not), Charles Shannon as a beautiful romantic poet, and many photographs, notably those by Howard Coster (see p. 9), reveal his intellectual toughness, while the bronze head by Kathleen Scott portrays his intensity.

KATHARINE TYNAN (1859–1931)

Born in Dublin, Katharine Tynan was encouraged in her writing by her father. Her first book of poems, the very successful *Louise de la Vallière* (1885), was followed by *Shamrocks* (1887) and *Ballads and Poems* (1891), all of which reflect her interest in Irish themes and her strong Catholicism. She met Yeats in 1885, and they became close friends, sharing common hopes for Irish literature. At her father's farm outside Dublin Yeats met Irish Catholic writers and editors who published his work. When the Yeats family moved from Dublin to London in 1887 he and she wrote frequently to each other (and about each other's work in various periodicals).

Katharine Tynan married Henry Hinkson in 1893 and they lived in London until 1911, when he became a magistrate in Co. Mayo. Although an admirer of Parnell in her youth, she had no sympathy with republicanism and moved to England after her husband's death in 1919. John Butler Yeats portrayed her as a severe young woman (his son William Butler Yeats later called her 'a plain woman'), but this portrait by Powys Evans conveys her strength of character. Tynan was not to fulfil her early poetic promise: for financial reasons she had to work under pressure, and the result was over a hundred novels, twelve collections of stories, three plays and four volumes of memoirs.

KATHARINE TYNAN
Powys Evans

GEORGE WILLIAM RUSSELL, Marion Broadhead

GEORGE WILLIAM RUSSELL (1867–1935)

Russell wrote and painted under the pseudonym 'AE'. He was educated at Rathmines School, Dublin, and at the School of Art, where his friendship with Yeats began in 1884. Russell began to see visions and to paint what he saw; he became a theosophist, poetry, painting and mysticism uniting in him, and this portrait conveys his friendly, enthusiastic visionary nature. Described as 'an unsuspecting apostle of the literary revival', his first book of poems, *Homeward Songs by the Way* (1894), evoked contemplative spiritual moods, and subsequent volumes continued this strain.

Thorough-going mystic though he was, Russell proved himself a highly capable organiser, setting up co-operative banks in the west of Ireland. George Moore paid tribute to his efficiency and kindness, describing something of his influential role in Dublin society in *Hail and Farewell*. Russell's practicality was a great help to Yeats when the National Theatre was being transformed into a more professional limited company. By then both held different views about what drama should be and their attitudes to poetry had altered. Yeats thought Russell was driven by moral and religious abstractions in his writings, overtolerant to amateurs and young poets. Russell's encouragement was somewhat uncritical, as the inclusions in his anthology *New Songs* (1904) demonstrate, although as editor of the *Irish Homestead*, the weekly organ of the Irish Co-operative Movement, he published from 1905 younger writers such as Padraic Colum and James Joyce.

Russell had supported the new Irish Free State in the *Irish Statesman* (which he edited from 1923 to 1930), but his nationalism was not militant and he was disillusioned by de Valera's election in 1932. Deeply depressed by the deaths of his wife and Sir Horace Plunkett (the founder of the Irish Co-operative Movement) Russell left Ireland in 1933. His unselfish, abundantly generous, idealistic life had explored the nature of inspiration, something disarmingly related in his *Candle of Vision* (1918).

Douglas Hyde (1860–1949)

The son of a Church of Ireland rector, Hyde grew up in Co. Sligo and then at Frenchpark in Co. Roscommon, where he learnt Irish from local speakers, arriving at Trinity College, Dublin, with a passionate enthusiasm for the language. He began to publish poems in Irish, and collected texts, manuscripts, songs and stories, thinking a knowledge of Irish would increase national self-respect as people recovered their own culture. In Dublin he got to know the influential old Fenian John O'Leary, as well as O'Grady and Yeats in 1885.

Elected President of the National Literary Society on its formation in 1892, his inaugural address, *On the Necessity for De-Anglicising Ireland*, became a key document in the development of Ireland's cultural independence.

Hyde's first book, a collection of Irish folk tales, riddles and rhymes, appeared in 1889. The next year, in *Beside the Fire*, he provided a new kind of anthology of folk tales with Irish texts faced by translations into Hiberno-English which successfully brought out Irish idiom and syntax, a model for the language later used by Lady Gregory and Synge. Yeats called it the coming of a new power into literature.

Hyde worked energetically: after *The Story of Early Gaelic Literature* (1895) came the impressive, indeed magisterial, *A Literary History of Ireland* (1899). His rigorous scholarship promoted the standing of Celtic culture in European history.

By the early 1900s Hyde's energies were increasingly occupied by the Gaelic League; a co-founder, he was the first president. The League's aims were to revive Irish as a living language and he did much to make it the strongest organisation in Ireland.

Douglas Hyde incurred some hostility, from Unionists and even from people sympathetic to his aims, as well as some ridicule. Moore remarked that his speeches in English were so incoherent it was easy to see why he wanted to make Irish the first official language, and called his Irish 'a torrent of dark muddied stuff like porter'. The language movement, however, acquired acceptability, indeed a momentum Hyde could not have foreseen in his perhaps politically naive insistence that it was not involved in politics. Indeed, at the League's *Ard Feis* (general meeting) in 1915 a radical politically motivated motion was carried, making the League's

objective a free Gaelic-speaking Ireland, and Hyde resigned.

Appointed Professor of Modern Irish at University College, Dublin, in 1908, Hyde held the post until he retired in 1932. His portrait by Sean O'Sullivan shows us the academic at ease, neither critical nor quarrelsome, but someone who has been popular, persuasive and 'a cajoler of crowds', who achieved much and enjoyed life.

Thereafter, Hyde's professional life occupied most of his attention, and recognition of what he had achieved (largely between 1893 and 1908) in shaping Ireland's consciousness of and confidence in its language and traditions was his uncontested election in 1938 as the first President of Ireland.

LADY ISABELLA AUGUSTA GREGORY (1852–1932)

Augusta Persse was born and grew up in 'a hive of life', Roxborough House, Co. Galway. When almost twenty-eight she escaped from the hearty life of her large family into a more intellectual, cultured milieu, marrying Sir William Gregory, a widower nearly thirty years her senior, who had inherited the neighbouring estate of Coole.

LADY ISABELLA AUGUSTA GREGORY
Mrs Jopling, 1893

When Sir William died in 1892 Lady Gregory ran the Coole estate. She wanted to share in the cultural nationalism Yeats and Hyde were promoting and she created a hospitable ambience at Coole, inviting many authors and artists there. In 1897 Yeats, Edward Martyn and she formed the idea of establishing a theatre for Irish drama. Full of energy, she set herself to gathering financial support for the project.

Lady Gregory's readiness to help others led her to encourage Yeats to join her in collecting folklore and traditions in the Galway countryside, thinking the fresh air and exercise would enable him to recover from the strain of living in London on the very little money he made from his books and journalism. Their work resulted in her *Visions and Beliefs in the West of Ireland* (1920). This portrait by Mrs Jopling, while not perhaps conveying Lady Gregory's capacity for humour, shows splendidly the generosity, firmness and nobility of her character.

After editing *Literary Ideals in Ireland* (1901), Lady Gregory translated and ordered material from the Ulster cycle of tales; *Cuchulain of Muirthemne* (1902) is an effective narrative, freshly conveying the spirit and idiom of the tales in the Hiberno-English spoken by the people of Kiltartan, a village near Coole. Her *Gods and Fighting Men* (1904) handled material from the mythological and Fenian cycles with equal success.

It was not only as director, play-reader and fundraiser that she contributed to the Abbey Theatre's success for, realising the need for a counter-balance to the theatre's poetic tragedies, she set herself to writing one-act comedies. She wrote forty plays, investing comic situations with extravagances of ideas or language, and setting her folk-history plays at crucial moments of Irish history. A good fighter, Lady Gregory defended Synge's *Playboy* against nationalists and Irish-American opponents during the Abbey tour of America, successfully engaged the Dublin censor in order to stage Shaw's *The Shewing-up of Blanco Posnet* in 1909, and was tireless in her efforts to get her nephew Sir Hugh Lane's Impressionist pictures back to Dublin after he went down with the *Lusitania*.

Some of the *raison d'être* of her life had vanished when her son, an RFC pilot, was shot down in 1918, but her last years were nobly celebrated by Yeats in poems set in Coole praising her powerful character, 'the scene well set and excellent company'.

GEORGE MOORE (1852–1933)

❦

Born at Moore Hall in Co. Mayo, a large house built by his great grand-father, George Moore inherited the house and estate in 1870. The income he received from it was enough for him to go to Paris with the idea of becoming a painter. He entered the Ecole des Beaux-Arts, then worked at Jullian's Academy for a time before deciding he was not good enough to succeed as an artist.

By 1876 he began to think of being a writer. In France he was influenced by such authors as Théophile Gautier, Charles Baudelaire and Stéphane Mallarmé, who regarded art as necessarily divorced from the common affairs of mankind. Mallarmé introduced Moore to café life and his real education began. Yeats described him at this period as sitting in some café 'a man carved out of a turnip, looking out of astonished eyes'. His unusual appearance, pale yellow hair, grey-green eyes and a delicate pink complexion, a receding chin beneath a straggling moustache and a long neck rising from sloping shoulders, is well caught in his portraits. Both Manet and Degas drew him: both seemed to Moore God-like, fifty years on 'his eyes were still dazzled' by Manet's painting, an enthusiasm captured in Sir William Orpen's painting of him in *Homage to Manet* (Manchester City Art Gallery). Moore's friend Henry Tonks also portrayed him in his later years, not always to Moore's satisfaction, but he conveys his pink complexion well, as well as his child-like curiosity.

The Land War in Ireland forced Moore to leave Paris and live frugally in London, writing articles about Zola and French naturalistic novels. He remarked that he had something to say though he did not know how to say it. Oscar Wilde said Moore conducted his education in public, taking seven years to discover grammar, then after it the paragraph. Told about the subjunctive he was delighted with it: 'Oh, I would give *anything* to be able to use the subjunctive. If it be; if it rain; how wonderful!'

Moore's first novel was published in 1883; six others followed before *Esther Waters* (1894) established him as the most original novelist of the day. It was about servants and drew upon his knowledge of horseracing, based upon his father's racing stable, and its effects. An earlier autobiographical book, *Confessions of a Young Man* (1888), giving his impression of aestheticism, was designed to shock and surprise his readers. He gained respect, however, by the critical essays collected in *Impressions and*

Opinions (1891) and in *Modern Painting* (1893)– warm-hearted, knowledgeable appreciations of the paintings of the French Impressionists.

Disgusted by English jingoism over the Boer War, Moore returned to Ireland in 1899, proclaiming in Dublin the coincidence of great art with national re-awakening. He decided to take a hand in the new Irish dramatic movement, becoming the third director of the Irish Literary Theatre (which lasted until 1901), aiding his co-directors, Yeats and his own cousin, Edward Martyn, in the production of their plays.

GEORGE MOORE, Henry Tonks, 1920

Moore approved highly of the Irish Co-operative Movement begun by Sir Horace Plunkett and of George Russell who administered it and helped Moore to settle into Dublin. The purposes of the Gaelic League attracted him and he developed a strong if short-lived enthusiasm for Irish.

Hail and Farewell (Ave, Salve and *Vale*, 1911–14) records Moore's ten years in Dublin: a brilliantly comic portrait of major figures of the literary movement, it treats facts and chronology in accordance with Moore's artistic purposes, conveying his wide-eyed wonder in an ironic, provocatively malicious and mischievously entertaining panorama of Dublin life.

Before the book's publication, Moore left Dublin for London, his last residence, where his continuing, still developing abilities showed in more novels, while the autobiographical *Conversations in Ebury Street* (1924), added to a magnificently varied achievement.

JOHN MILLINGTON SYNGE (1871–1909)

A member of a closely knit Dublin evangelical family of landowning stock, Synge lost his capacity for belief after reading Darwin as a child. After graduating at Trinity College, Dublin, he studied music in Germany, hoping to become a professional musician. He moved to Paris where, like George Moore before him, he altered his plans, now aiming to be a writer. The turning-point in his life was meeting Yeats in Paris in 1896, for Yeats urged him to go to the Aran Islands to find entirely new subject-matter there. Synge, who had a good knowledge of Irish, made five visits to these islands in Galway Bay between 1898 and 1902. He was taken with the vitality of the Irish-speaking islanders, their stoic endurance and the exuberant vigour of the English they spoke 'with a slight foreign intonation'.

His haunting, elegiac one-act tragedy *Riders to the Sea* (1904) employs an English based on Gaelic syntax and on what Synge heard in the islands and in the isolated glens and valleys of Co. Wicklow. The first production of his powerful *In the Shadow of the Glen* in 1903 caused controversy, Irish

JOHN MILLINGTON SYNGE
John Butler Yeats, 1905

30

nationalists being unduly sensitive about the loveless marriages among country people it depicted.

Synge began to gain international recognition, and became closely involved with the administration of the Abbey Theatre as co-director with Yeats and Lady Gregory. He read and sometimes rewrote others' plays, as well as directing them; he soothed the players when Yeats irritated them; he acted as go-between when Miss Horniman, Yeats's English friend who had financed the purchase of the theatre, and Willie Fay, the director and stage manager, were at loggerheads; he accompanied the players on tours in Ireland and England. And he fell in love with a young Abbey actress, Molly Algood (whose stage name was Máire O'Neill). It was a stormy relationship; he wrote poems of delight to her, but his letters record quarrels and misunderstandings.

These letters also convey the difficulties encountered in writing his masterpiece *The Playboy of the Western World*, which provoked riots in the theatre when it was staged in 1907, nationalists regarding it as a slur on Irish womanhood. Lady Gregory called in the police on the second night, and Yeats returned to Dublin to hold a famous public meeting to discuss the play and insist upon its continued performance. It is a richly robust contrast between romanticism and reality, a *tour-de-force* of imaginative expression shaped by Synge's powerful poetic mind; it contains comedy, farce and the tragedy of Pegeen Mike discovering she has lost the playboy whom she had herself helped to create.

Deirdre of the Sorrows was written when Synge was ill and worried about poverty. Conscious of the shortness of human life, he had turned to saga material, regarding the Deirdre theme as an expression of life at its most intense. He and Molly planned to marry in the autumn of 1907 but postponed the date until he could recover from an operation to remove swollen glands from his neck, the symptoms of Hodgkin's Disease. Another operation in 1908 discovered an inoperable tumour, and he died at the age of thirty-eight, still working on the unfinished *Deirdre*. W. B. Yeats wrote well of this ironic, silent, always observant man, whose withdrawn nature is well brought out here in the portrait by J. B. Yeats: 'Noble art was always passionate and in Synge's passion, asceticism, stoicism and ecstasy all came together'.

GEORGE BERNARD SHAW (1856–1950)

S haw described his Dublin family as 'downstarts'. When his mother and
sisters moved to London in 1876 he too sought its larger stage, like
many Irish dramatists before him: his plays follow in the social comedy
tradition of Farquhar, Congreve, Steele, Goldsmith, Sheridan and Wilde.
Shaw established his reputation as an art, music and drama critic, writing
superbly clear and cogent prose. An early member of the Fabian Society,
he attacked social evils, injustice and irregularity, reversing stereotyped
situations in novel, witty, paradoxical and challenging plays. There are
many portraits of Shaw, whose interest in photography was awakened
when Emery Walker photographed him in 1888; Walker's photographs
reveal a man alert, aggressively challenging and quizzical, a master of the
paradox. Ten years later Shaw bought a Kodak camera and began to photograph himself (there is even a nude self-portrait) and his wife.

His career as dramatist, self-publicist, free-thinker and social moralist
extended to over fifty plays and won him the Nobel Prize in 1925. Shaw's
connection with the literary revival was somewhat peripheral; true, Yeats
commissioned his first commercial success, *John Bull's Other Island* (1904).
A play questioning accepted ideas about the Irish and English characters,
this was not produced at the Abbey. But *The Shewing-up of Blanco Posnet*
(1909), refused a licence by the English censor on the grounds of its
alleged blasphemy, was produced, despite the threat of the theatre's
patent being revoked. Shaw's other Irish play, *O'Flaherty VC* (1915),
designed to aid recruiting for the British Army but with a hero exclaiming
'no war is right' and presenting Ireland as 'unmitigated hell', was not produced for fear of the rioting it might provoke. Seven of his other plays
were, however, performed at the Abbey between 1916 and 1917. In 1932
he was unanimously elected President of the Irish Academy of Letters, an
organisation that brought together all kinds of Irish writers; he liked its
opposition to the Irish censorship. In these later years he was portrayed
benignly – and wisely – enjoying life.

GEORGE BERNARD SHAW, Emery Walker

EDITH OENONE SOMERVILLE AND VIOLET FLORENCE MARTIN, unknown photographer

EDITH OENONE SOMERVILLE (1858–1949) AND VIOLET FLORENCE MARTIN (1862–1915)

Superb writers of fiction, these two cousins met in 1886 at Edith's family home Castletownshend, Co. Cork, while Violet was on a visit from Ross House, near Oughterard, Co. Galway. Edith had studied painting, and Violet had published various political articles. They wrote their first novel *An Irish Cousin* (1889) under the joint pseudonym Somerville and Ross. They had intended a sensational Gothic novel but in the process of writing discovered their true metier, portraying in five novels and three volumes of short stories the tragi-comedy of Ascendancy Big Houses in decline. After her cousin's death Edith wrote five more novels, believing her cousin's spirit was helping her.

Their masterpiece, *The Real Charlotte* (1894), is impressive in the scope of its comic irony and subtle indications of social nuances, 'the more knife-edged slice of sarcasm' coming from Violet Martin while the loving descriptions of the countryside can probably be attributed to Edith's painterly eye. The story centres upon Charlotte Mullen, a ruthless, greedy and passionate woman driven by a desire for revenge; the narration is compelling, the dialogue makes the atmospheric picture of Irish life vivid and convincing.

The pair's other great success arose from a different impulse, its comedy founded upon a deadpan style. The Irish RM stories – *Some Experiences of an Irish RM* (1899), *Further Experiences of an Irish RM* (1908) and *In Mr Knox's Country* (1915) – centre round a worthy Englishman appointed Resident Magistrate in south-west Ireland where he is often baffled by the deviousness and social complexities of a horse-centred society: often gulled, he – like his creators – enjoys the eccentricity of a wide range of characters in this ramshackle society, from the autocratic Lady Knox to her inventive nephew Flurry Knox, horse-coper incarnate, from the dashing Bobbie Bennett to Mrs Cadogan and Skipper whose idiosyncratic Hiberno-English speech is lively and original.

The photograph portrait of the cousins suggests their close collaboration, their different personalities, Edith more active as befitted a future Master of Foxhounds, Violet short-sighted, often nervously exhausted, but also a fearless rider. Anglo-Irish in their detachment, Somerville and Ross portrayed an Ireland that was passing.

LORD DUNSANY (1878–1957)

E dward John Moreton Drax Plunkett, whose family settled in Ireland in the twelfth century, was the 18th Baron, inheriting Dunsany Castle and the family estate in Co. Meath in 1899. He fought in the Boer War and the First World War. He was a big-game hunter, sportsman and traveller, something of whose autocratic manner and searching glance is caught by this portrait. An impressively tall man, he wrote standing at his desk. Oliver St John Gogarty, who regarded him as 'the only living man who could write romantic prose', described him warmly in *As I Was Going Down Sackville Street*: 'golden evenings in Dunsany in the mellow lamp-light before the great fire, listening to the latest lyric recited or read in that vivid and pleasant accent of his. Exquisite language, excellent verse.'

Dunsany created a fantasy world with an elaborate mythology – not for nothing had he been encouraged by George Russell – in *The Gods of Pegana* (1905), *The Sword of Welleran* (1908) and *Tales of Wonder* (1916), effectively employing a biblical style in accounts of the cities Babbulkund and Perdonaris. Sardonic humour informed his Jorkins stories, five volumes published between 1931 and 1954 dealing with a good-humoured clubman who tells fanciful, indeed incredible stories. Dunsany's funniest book is *My Talks with Dean Spanley* (1936), in which a bland clergyman who has had too much wine reverts to a previous existence as a spaniel.

Following Russell's example, Dunsany encouraged younger writers, notably Francis Ledwidge and Mary Lavin: he wrote an introduction to Ledwidge's *Songs of the Fields* (1915), found him a publisher and edited his posthumous poems in 1919. He also wrote an introduction to Mary Lavin's *Tales of Bective Bridge* (1942). Dunsany's work included travel books, essays and three volumes of autobiography.

Lord Dunsany, unknown photographer, *c.*1930

FRANCIS LEDWIDGE (1887–1917)

Born at Slane, Co. Meath, Ledwidge was a labourer from the age of twelve; he became a road-ganger and was turned down by the girl he loved because she considered the job too lowly. He recorded his frustration in poems that continued to mourn the death of their love after Ellie Vaughan had married and died.

Ledwidge stiffened his romantic talent by reading Irish in translation, subsequently making use of internal rhyming and assonance (the latter very effective in his 'Lament for Thomas MacDonagh', an academic and author executed for his part in the 1916 Rising). Hoping to develop a career as a journalist he became Secretary to a Labour union, founded a corps of Volunteers and enlisted in the Royal Inniskilling Fusiliers in 1914. Ledwidge survived Gallipoli but was killed at Ypres in 1917.

Lord Dunsany selected and found a publisher for *Songs of the Fields* (1915), limpid poems reminiscent of those of the English poet John Clare,

full of delight in the details of the Meath countryside. Ledwidge's poetry shows some influences of Keats and exhibits a melancholia, possibly deriving from the example of the Georgian poets. *Songs of Peace* (1917), published posthumously, was succeeded by *Last Songs* (1918), again selected by Dunsany, who praised Ledwidge for having the great ideas and conceptions of a poet, for seeing 'the vast figures, the giant forces and elemental powers, striving among the hills'. This portrait suggests the psychic, religious, meditative nature of an idealistic yet essentially practical poet.

FRANCIS LEDWIDGE
Unknown photographer, *c.*1914

Eimar O'Duffy (1893–1935)

A Dubliner, Eimar O'Duffy was educated at Stonyhurst and University College, Dublin, where he qualified as a dentist. He never practised but wrote plays and joined the Irish Republican Brotherhood and the Irish Volunteers. His first novel *The Wasted Island* (1919) is probably the first disillusioned view of the Easter Rising of 1916. After losing his post in the Department of External Affairs O'Duffy moved to London in 1925 and maintained his family by journalism. Despite increasing ill health, O'Duffy wrote three detective novels between 1932 and 1935, in order to relieve his precarious financial position. He added to his dislike of the bourgeois state

Eimar O'Duffy
Lafayette, 10 December 1926

a strongly anti-clerical, often sardonic humour. He died before completing a projected autobiography, *The Portrait Gallery*, which was destroyed at his request.

O'Duffy's best-known work, *King Goshawk of the Birds* (1926), the first volume of a trilogy, inserted Irish mythological characters into a modern context, criticising capitalism with inventive irony and some mock-heroic material, anticipating the later work of Flann O'Brien. *Life and Money* (1932), based on Social Credit (a populist right-wing movement), offered reasons and possible remedies for the Depression.

JAMES STEPHENS, Mary Duncan, *c.*1915

JAMES STEPHENS (?1882–1950)

B orn in a Dublin he described as poor, Protestant and athletic, Stephens was brought up in an orphanage after his father died and his mother remarried. When young, he said, he entered into a Dublin poor, Catholic and Gaelic. He began to earn his living as a solicitor's clerk in 1896 extending his Dublin to one he called poor, artistic and political. Then, he added, he made a Dublin for himself.

Stephens's first volume of poetry, *Insurrections* (1909), expressed disgust and anger at the conditions of Dublin slum life. He became interested in William Blake and in Theosophy (beliefs based upon the writings of Brahminism and Buddhism, but denying the existence of a personal god). George Russell introduced him to Yeats and Lady Gregory, and Stephens began to study Irish seriously.

Two novels were published in 1912, *The Charwoman's Daughter* and *The Crock of Gold*. The first blended romantic dreaming and realism as Mary Makepeace considers her two suitors, a policeman and a lodger. *The Crock of Gold*, a highly idiosyncratic mixture of parody and philosophy, brought Stephens fame. Stephens had Yeats, Russell and Synge in mind when he brought the Celtic gods Angus Og and Pan into an Ireland where the false values of urban life were threatening pastoral innocence. This subtly narrated story of Caitlin, the heroine, growing into sexual maturity, expresses an ultimate vision of gender giving way to the collective wisdom which is true freedom. Stephens was capable of profound thought, although he disguised this with whimsical counterpointing, the comedy rooted in an unexpected and very effective matter-of-factness.

Stephens shared a delight in language, parody and impiety with Joyce, who asked him to finish *Finnegans Wake* should he be unable to do so himself. Stephens valued the lively Dublin speech of *Finnegans Wake*; he was himself a fine talker, his conversational brilliance captured in talks he gave for the BBC, published in *James Seamus and Jacques* (1964). Katharine Tynan described him as 'ready to roar down an opponent in a discussion . . . he was an intemperate talker to match AE [George Russell]'. Mary Duncan's casual representation was made around 1915 while she was teaching etching in Dublin, the year also that Stephens took up the registrarship of the National Gallery of Ireland. The lithograph catches the informal and very likeable, lively side of his character.

LIAM O'FLAHERTY (1896–1984)

A man of action as well as novelist and short-story writer, O'Flaherty was born on Inishmore, the largest of the Aran Islands. He abandoned studies for the priesthood to join the Irish Guards in 1915. Wounded in 1917, he suffered from depression and was discharged a year later. In the Irish Civil War he joined the Republicans and then took up radical politics. His first novel, *My Neighbour's Wife*, appeared in 1923, and was followed by *The Black Soul* (1924), *The Informer* (1925), *Mr Gilhooley* (1926) and *The Assassin* (1928).

O'Flaherty's dark, violent realism – seen as a reaction against the literary revival's romanticism – has, however, a strongly romantic element. *A Tourist's Guide to Ireland* (1930) recorded an irascible dislike of priests and politicians, whom he saw as oppressing the peasantry, about whom he wrote excellent short stories in Irish, his explosive genius at its best when compressed within this form. A series of mental breakdowns in the thirties led to the self-exploration and frustration recorded in three autobiographies. In 1932 O'Flaherty turned to Aran subjects in *Skerett*, another powerful novel equalled in its effectiveness by *Famine* (1937), the first of a turbulent trilogy about the development of modern Irish nationalism.

Two of his three autobiographical volumes, *Two Years* (1930) and *Shame the Devil* (1934) are most readable. To a certain extent they indicate an ability to control the outward signs of inner disturbances well, his writing acting as a safety valve, if not always an efficient one. In his last years he became something of a recluse.

The portrait gives an excellent impression of O'Flaherty, whose own emotional turbulence was matched by a capacity for endurance, summed up in his remark that 'you have to go through life with a shell bursting in your head'.

LIAM O'FLAHERTY, Howard Coster, 1935

SEAN O'CASEY, Wolfgang Suschitzky, 1955

SEAN O'CASEY (1880–1964)

O'Casey began work as a labourer at fourteen. He joined various charitable, social and political organisations, leaving the Citizen Army in 1914, and writing its history in 1919. *The Shadow of a Gunman,* which debunked the heroic reputation of the IRA's gunmen, was produced by the Abbey Theatre in 1923.

Juno and the Paycock followed the next year, the Abbey's most successful play so far, its tragi-comic action set in the Dublin slums in the period of the Civil War, employing the vigorous language spoken so spontaneously there. Juno's endurance and courage are contrasted with the boastful, drunken irresponsibility of her husband 'Captain' Boyle and his parasitic companion Joxer Daly, two brilliantly achieved comic characters. O'Casey attacks the inhumanity of political abstractions, the masculine bravado and vanity against which he sets the genuine bravery of the non-combatants, mainly patient, enduring women.

The Plough and the Stars (1926) was set in the period of the Easter Rising of 1916. Again, O'Casey contrasted the heady platitudes of patriotic rhetoric with the realities of violence. Too near the traumatic events that had occurred between 1916 and 1923 for the Dublin audience, the play was greeted by riots, and O'Casey moved to England.

When the Abbey rejected the first play he wrote after moving, an expressionist anti-war play, *The Silver Tassie* (1929), O'Casey decided he would live permanently in England. He did, however, return to Ireland with gusto in his six volumes of autobiography (1939–54), the first two of which are the most effective, with their account of life in Dublin slums; there is a certain amount of self-indulgence in these volumes, but in their best moments the autobiographies of this major dramatist are vivid and rewarding. Highly sensitive, O'Casey could react violently; indeed George Russell once described him to Yeats as a person not to be met with in ordinary controversy: 'He is like one of those fighters who keep to no rules, but bite, kick in the stomach and try to gouge out the eyes of the person they fight with'. O'Casey became milder, and more gracious as he grew older – his marriage to the actress Eileen Reynolds was very successful and is well described in her book *Sean* (1971) – and this greater ease and benignity is reflected in the photograph opposite.

DENIS JOHNSTON (1901–84)

While O'Casey had contrasted men's vain heroics with women's stoic courage, a Dublin barrister, Denis Johnston, wrote some expressionist plays, the first of which, *The Old Lady Says No!* (1929), contrasts the past idealism of the revolutionary Robert Emmet with the realities of life in the new Irish Free State. *The Moon on the Yellow River* (1931) deals with the effect of a struggle between Free-Staters and Republicans on a power station. Expressionism allowed Johnston to exhibit disillusion with nationalist ideals and later show his highly critical views of the legal system in *The Golden Cuckoo* (1939), and in a play of 1936, reworked as *Strange Occurrence on Ireland's Eye* (1956), which questioned the very nature of justice.

Like George Bernard Shaw, Denis Johnston wanted to engage his audience in thinking about the issues his plays raised. He moved to the BBC in 1938; his experiences as one of their war correspondents, evocatively recounted in *Nine Rivers from Jordan* (1953), revealed a deep moral and philosophical outlook, a vein further explored in *The Brazen Horn* (1976). In 1946 he left the BBC, teaching in various American universities and completing *In Search of Swift* (1959), largely about Swift's parentage and his complex relationships with women, particularly 'Stella' and 'Vanessa'.

This bold painting of Denis Johnston by the Irish artist and illustrator Norah McGuinness, who had worked in Paris, London and New York before settling in Dublin, resembles her landscapes and abstracts in its hard, strong angular lines; it catches her subject's courage and conveys the strength of his intellect and character – he became a very charismatic academic and conversationalist. Johnston did not, however, consider America as a country for conversation, and spent his last fifteen years in Dublin. His own attitudes had been learned, he said, from George Bernard Shaw, 'the same scepticism of greatness, and a profound dislike of anything that savours of magic'.

DENIS JOHNSTON, Norah McGuinness, *c.*1940–50

KATE O'BRIEN, Mary O'Neill, 1936

KATE O'BRIEN (1897–1974)

The well-to-do family from which Kate O'Brien came was not unlike the one she described rising from poverty in her first novel *Without My Cloak* (1931). Born and bred in Limerick, she was educated there in a convent run by French nuns, and later went to University College, Dublin. O'Brien did not settle to being a full-time writer until her play *Distinguished Villa* achieved success in London in 1926.

Her romantic yet realistic novels explored the reactions of heroines to conflicts between their moral upbringing and sexual passion, portraying not only their searching for love and individual freedom but their need for education. Subtle in her early feminism, Kate O'Brien was also ahead of her time in her Europeanism – as a young woman she had spent some time in Spain as a governess – tracing Ireland's links to continental civilisation. *Mary Lavelle* (1936) was banned by the Irish censorship, as was *The Land of Spices* (1941), about a nun's spiritual development. Kate O'Brien was also banned from Spain for many years because of what she wrote about General Franco and his followers in a travel book, *Farewell to Spain* (1938).

KATE O'BRIEN, Howard Coster

Portraits of O'Brien reveal that she was not without hauteur as a person; she did not suffer fools gladly, but could be either charmingly humorous or completely crushing. She was an original writer; her best novel, *That Lady* (1946), tracing the conflict between Aña de Mendoza and Philip II of Spain, provides yet another celebration of the individual's capacity to resist tyranny.

SEAN O'FAOLAIN (b. JOHN WHELAN, 1900–91)

Two Cork writers, Sean O'Faolain and Frank O'Connor, whose short stories were major achievements in their impressive literary careers, came under the influence of Daniel Corkery (1878–1964) who taught at University College, Cork, and was himself an artist, short-story writer of some distinction, novelist and dramatist. Corkery's book on eighteenth–century Gaelic writers, *The Hidden Ireland* (1924), and his *Synge and Anglo-Irish Literature* (1931) provided criticism influential in its own time, though O'Faolain reacted strongly against its restrictive Irish-Irish views of the literary movement.

An idealist, O'Faolain played an active part in the Civil War himself, but became disillusioned when his vision was not matched by the results achieved. He spent some years in the United States and England before returning to Ireland in 1933. The best of his novels, *Bird Alone*, was published in 1936; he wrote biographies, travel books and several volumes of excellently crafted short stories, collected in three volumes between 1980 and 1982.

In 1940 O'Faolain founded *The Bell*, an influential monthly dealing with literary, political and cultural issues, editing it with panache for six years. He intensely disliked the orthodoxies of the Gaelic Ireland de Valera was trying to create, the repressive anti-intellectualism symbolised by the censorship, and the conservative nature of Irish Catholicism.

Sean O'Faolain's portrait indicates his searching glance; he got to the point quickly and incisively – his short stories were more effective than his novels, as a result – yet he was capable of deep and searching thought. His intellectual independence informs *The Irish* (1948); aware of the deadening effects of traditionalism, he influenced many younger Irish writers, his own intensifying human sympathy prompting him to use fresh approaches to fight for the expression of individual free will.

SEAN O'FAOLAIN, Howard Coster

FRANK O'CONNOR
(pseudonym of MICHAEL O'DONOVAN, 1903–66)

After being interned as a Republican in the Civil War, Frank O'Connor became a librarian; his first volume of short stories, *Guests of the Nation* (1931), was followed the next year by a novel, *The Saint and Mary Kate*. He became friendly with Yeats, joined in the setting-up of the Irish Academy of Letters and contributed to the Cuala Press, run by one of Yeats's sisters, a volume of fine translations from the Irish, *The Wild Bird's Nest* (1932). He continued to write short stories, striving successfully to narrate them as if they were spoken aloud.

With much of his writing banned as indecent by the Irish censorship, O'Connor grew disenchanted with Irish life and taught in American universities for nine years before returning to Ireland in 1960. His deep voice made his lecturing and broadcasting memorable. Out of his university teaching came three critical studies, on the novel, the short story and the history of Irish literature, the last, *The Backward Look* (1967), being the most impressive. O'Connor continued with his excellent translations of Gaelic poetry in *Kings, Lords and Commons* (1959) and *A Golden Treasury of Irish Poetry, 600–1200* (edited with David Greene, 1959). This portrait shows the sharply contemplative look he bestowed on life and literature; his own writing was based upon a deep sense of humour allied to fine craftsmanship and an ability not only to appreciate Gaelic tradition but to bring to that appreciation a sensibility nurtured upon a reflective knowledge and enjoyment of European literature.

FRANK O'CONNOR, unknown photographer

JOYCE CARY (1888–1957)

One of many Irish writers who settled in England, Cary went to Oxford after studying art in Paris and Edinburgh. He served with the Red Cross in the Balkan War in 1912 and the Colonial Service in Nigeria, being wounded in service in the Cameroons during the war. He settled in Oxford in 1920, writing, among other work, five novels about Africa and two trilogies about England (including his famous *The Horse's Mouth* of 1944). His childhood holidays at his grandmother's house in Co. Donegal inspired his magnificently joyous novel *A House for Children* (1941), while *Castle Corner* (1938)

JOYCE CARY, self-portrait, 1956

had linked his sense of the past with change, showing Cary's belief that a balance could be achieved between imaginative freedom and collective responsibility.

His training as an artist led Cary to seize upon important details – his self-portrait gives an economical but realistic impression of his distinguished features. Even in his last years when he was suffering from motor-neurone disease he gave the impression of a person persisting in lofty thought, for Cary reflected in an original way upon modern life. He was particularly concerned with changes in society and with the capacity of individuals to make their own choices, despite being members of mass civilisation, which he viewed the better for his observation of tribal life in Africa. Cary wrote especially well about creativity, the speed of change, courage in women and the nature of power.

ELIZABETH BOWEN (1899–1973)

Like Joyce Cary, Elizabeth Bowen came of a family that settled in Ireland in the seventeenth century. In *Bowen's Court* (1942) she wrote of the family house in Co. Cork which she inherited in 1930. She recorded her early Dublin childhood in *Seven Winters* (1942). Her childhood was unsettled after her father's mental instability became apparent in 1907 and her mother died in 1912. Her father remarried in 1918, and Elizabeth spent holidays in Bowen's Court. A romantic engagement, broken off by an interfering aunt in 1921, was followed by her marriage to the educationalist Alan Cameron in 1923. This lasted, despite her many subsequent affairs and her habit of excluding him from her circle of literary friends.

The striking portraits of Bowen mirror mainly an authority and a certain ruthlessness in her character. Her novels, often based closely upon her own life, include *The Last September* (1929), set in Ireland, her best being *The Heat of the Day* (1949), dealing with espionage and reflecting the stresses and strains of an intense wartime love affair. Elizabeth Bowen wrote well of betrayal and manipulation, probing below layers of social respectability, her short stories allowing her more scope for her often farouche yet always distinguished and distinctive style. Anglo-Irish in her ability to convey the qualities of life she knew in both Ireland and England, she was made a Companion of Literature in 1965.

ELIZABETH BOWEN, Howard Coster

ELIZABETH BOWEN, André Durand, 1969

JAMES JOYCE (1882–1941)

Joyce began to write seriously in 1904, the year he eloped from Dublin with Nora Barnacle to live in Pola, then Trieste. He had grown up in a family impoverished by his father's feckless conviviality, and was educated at Jesuit schools before graduating from University College, Dublin. He spent two brief periods in Paris, and some time school-teaching in Dublin. By 1904 Joyce had acquired most of the experience that went into his fiction *Dubliners* (1914), *Stephen Hero* (partly published posthumously in 1944), *A Portrait of the Artist as a Young Man* (1916), *Ulysses* (1922) and *Finnegans Wake* (1939).

In the stories of *Dubliners*, studies of frustration, inertia, alcoholism and conformity to the conventional values prescribed by the Irish Catholic Church, Joyce constantly drew upon knowledge and memories of Dublin, 'the centre of paralysis'. Against these confining forces he applied his radical, iconoclastic questioning mind, recording in the autobiographically based *Stephen Hero* and *A Portrait* the progress of Stephen Dedalus from infancy through troubled adolescence to his young manhood when he decides upon his vocation as artist, leaving Ireland to face the reality of experience. In rejecting home, fatherland, church, he chooses for defence 'silence, exile and cunning'.

Despite an early admiration for Yeats, Joyce disliked the absolutes of nationalism as much of those of Catholicism; he rejected the tenets of the literary movement. He had satirised the folk art and idealism of some revival writers in 'The Holy Office' of 1904, having by then written most of the delicate lyric poems of *Chamber Music* (1907), most of which have been set to music – some by Joyce himself, who had a fine tenor voice.

Joyce taught in a Berlitz school in Trieste until 1907; he and Nora had two children, and the family's financial situation was precarious as Joyce seemed set to repeat his father's excessive drinking, and his frequent house-moving. After interludes in Rome and Dublin and, during the war, in Zurich, the Joyces lived in Paris from 1920 until the Second World War.

His masterpiece, *Ulysses*, was published in 1922, and is considered by many the twentieth century's major work of fiction. Begun in 1914, it took on epic dimensions, many of its episodes parallel to portions of Homer's *Odyssey*. Leopold Bloom, a Jewish advertising canvasser, easygoing and tolerant, a modern Everyman, corresponds to Ulysses; his unfaithful wife Molly, earthy in her sensual sexual attitudes, to Penelope; and Stephen Dedalus (met earlier in *A Portrait*) who has rejected family, religion and mysticism, and is in search of a spiritual father as Bloom is of a spiritual son, to Telemachus. The novel is concentrated into eighteen hours of a Dublin day, portraying modern urban life as it impinges upon and is revealed in the thoughts, conscious and subconscious, and the doings of its main characters. Form and style were experimental: Joyce deployed the interior monologue (probably derived from the techniques of the eighteenth-century Irish-born Laurence Sterne) and used parodies of different literary styles to create an impersonal narrative with multiple viewpoints, employing psychological realism to portray the human spirit, imposing a structural order upon the flux of experience.

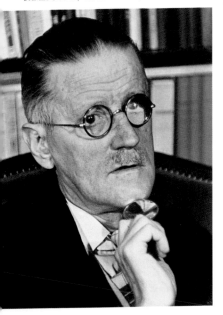

JAMES JOYCE, Gisèle Freund, 1939

In Paris Joyce was free to concentrate upon *Finnegans Wake* but troubles intervened: his daughter's schizophrenia, his own attacks of gastro-enteritis and, above all, his failing eyesight. He relied upon friends to read to him, one of whom was Samuel Beckett. It took Joyce seventeen years to complete *Finnegans Wake*, a multi-layered multilingual comic epic – which is at times very funny. It contains much arcane learning, philosophical universality and the strange fluxes of the dream world. It explores the concerns of HCE (Humphrey Chimpden Ear-wicker), ALP (Anna Livia Plurabelle) and their three children. Joyce regarded it as his most significant work.

FLANN O'BRIEN
(pseudonym of BRIAN O'NOLAN, 1911–66)

❧

At Swim Two-Birds, O'Brien's comic novel of 1939, is a blend of Irish tales and popular fiction, and owed much to Joyce's experimental techniques. Joyce used to recite passages from it admiringly. O'Brien, born in an Irish-speaking household at Strabane, Co. Tyrone, progressed from University College, Dublin, to the Irish Civil Service, where he eventually rose to be principal officer for town planning. As Myles na Gopaleen, he wrote, from 1940 to his death, a column called 'Cruiskeen Lawn' in the *Irish Times*, for whom this photograph was taken. For nearly a year the column was written largely in Irish; often couched in Dublin argot, it proved a successful satiric mixture: puns, paradoxes, parodies, advice and attacks on politicians and bureaucrats. After the publication of *At Swim Two-Birds* O'Brien failed to get his next novel *The Third Policeman* (1967), written in 1940, published, and, deeply disappointed, put it aside. In 1941 he wrote what is the blackest example of his humour, *An Béal Bocht*, which describes the fictitious Irish-speaking community of Corca Dorcha, satirising classic Gaelic autobiographies and academic attitudes to the Gaeltacht, the Irish-speaking areas. It did not achieve success until its appearance in an English version, *The Poor Mouth*, in 1964.

The forties and fifties were a dark time for O'Brien, whose frustrated irritability combined with excessive drinking led to his retirement from the civil service in 1953. *The Hard Life* (1961) was a best-seller, and O'Brien's confidence returned with *The Dalkey Archive* (1964), a burlesque satiric novel attacking schematic rational planning.

FLANN O'BRIEN, unknown photographer

SAMUEL BECKETT (1906–89)

❦

Like Joyce, Beckett decided to live in Paris, settling there in 1937, after teaching in Belfast, Paris and Dublin. His first novel, *Murphy* (1938), blended burlesque mockery of the literary revival with philosophical concepts, Murphy wanting to reach nothingness. Beckett wrote his second novel, *Watt* (1953), during the war, when he worked for the French Resistance, for which he was awarded the Croix de Guerre. Watt is a logical positivist, who cannot make sense of nothing, and the book illustrates the illogicality of human life.

Beckett's next three novels were written in French. *Molloy* (1951) is a novel of despair. *Malone Dies* (1956) employs black humour as Malone wonders why he is suffering; he is waiting for death, for nothing. *The Unnameable* (1959) has a main character with a lack of certainty about anything; the novel concludes with his wish to continue talking but disliking language. *How it is* (1964) is a minimalist work; none of Joyce's exuberant imaginative exploration of language here, words are reduced to a minimum, the novel's fragmented narratives conveying doubts about human existence.

Beckett put ideas about the division between 'the reality' and mind into dramatic form in his best-known work, *Waiting for Godot* (1954), an inconclusive play, witty, grotesque, stoical, challenging. Who is Godot for whom the tramps Estragon and Vladimir are waiting?

Further plays pursued minimalism. *Endgame* (1958) has two characters in ashbins, their son Hamm is blind and paralysed, and the servant Clov is able to walk but unable to sit down: a situation where nothing is known, nor indeed is likely to be. Beckett explored mime in *Act Without Words* (1958) and dance in *Quad* (written 1979). The process towards nothing increased in tempo. *Happy Days* (1961) has a character buried to the waist in act one and to the neck in act two, while in the monologue *Krapp's Last Tape* (1958) a character comments on a tape recording he'd made twenty years before. *Krapp* was succeeded by the 121-word *Come and Go* (1969) and *Not I* (1973), another monologue, in which only the actor's mouth is illuminated. Beckett was involved in the practicalities of theatre; as a director of his own plays, he wished to control the actors, restricting their movement, seeing a play as a total performance of rhythm, pattern and musicality, a point brought out in this portrait of

him directing at the Riverside Studios in London.

In 1969 Beckett was awarded the Nobel Prize for Literature. He was a questioner, deploying a cold intellect upon conditions of horror and pain, and his irony and wit go back to many of his Irish predecessors, with whose work he was impressively familiar. In Jane Bown's photograph (see p. 12), Beckett's face reflects an inner toughness, a capacity for enduring, a patience and stoicism; it is an unsentimental face, which harbours, as well as wit and irony, a regret for the aridity he saw in modern society.

SEAMUS HEANEY, Peter Edwards, 1987–8

Seamus Heaney (b. 1939)

Ireland's most recent Nobel Prize winner (in 1995), Heaney was brought up on a farm in Co. Derry. Educated at St Columb's College, Derry, and Queen's University, Belfast (where he taught for some years), he has been Professor of Poetry at Oxford and, since 1984, a Professor at Harvard University.

His first volume of poems, *Death of a Naturalist* (1966), emphasises the continuity of rural life as perceived by a child. Memory's layers are explored in *Door into the Dark* (1969). In *Wintering Out* (1972) Heaney has used the image of a ritual murder victim found in a Jutland bog to illuminate Irish parallels. *Field Work* (1979) marked a new assurance, exemplified in the Glanmore Sonnets about Heaney's life in Glanmore Cottage, Co. Wicklow. In *Station Island* (1984) he used the pilgrimage to Lough Derg to investigate his own literary and family ghosts. This portrait by Peter Edwards illustrates the relaxed personality of the poet; his is a genial character, and his largeness of vision is well captured here. Heaney is, however, a poet of detail: he uses it to convey deeper meanings. A confident, thoughtful poet and stimulating critic, he continues to share his thoughts and ideas easily: they are marked by a careful use of language which conveys an optimistic and welcome ease of mind, and this is a reminder of how much has been achieved in a little over a hundred years of independent Irish writing.

SEAMUS HEANEY, Mark Gerson, 1996

List of Illustrations

❧